Why Should I Nurse My Baby?

And Other Questions Mothers Ask About Breastfeeding

Pamela K. Wiggins, IBCLC
International Board Certified Lactation Consultant

NOTE: The author realizes that babies come in both sexes, but for the sake of simplicity, will refer to the baby as "he" throughout this booklet. She apologizes to all baby girls.

WHY SHOULD I NURSE MY BABY?
ISBN # 0-9623529-7-7
© Copyright 2009

For bulk ordering information:
L. A. Publishing, LLC
P. O. Box 773
Franklin, Virginia 23851
1-800-397-5833
804-744-6022 (Fax)
www.breastfeedingbooks.com

Illustrations: Jennifer Councill
Art Director: Eric Garofalo
Photos on pages 5, 43 and 61 courtesy of Texas Department of Health

Introduction

Some of the sweetest moments of your life will be when you are nursing your baby.

Congratulations on becoming a mother! This is an exciting time of your life and before your baby is born, you will need to make many choices for him. How you decide to feed him is very important. This book explains **why** breastfeeding is the best choice and **how** to be successful.

Breastfeeding is the normal way of feeding babies. Women have breastfed their babies since the beginning of mankind. In fact, it has only been in the last sixty years or so that mothers have fed their babies artificial baby milk.

That's when formula companies began advertising that formula was "just as good" as human milk. Many people, even doctors, believed them and breastfeeding went out of style for a long time. Most mothers today have not grown up in a world where breastfeeding is seen as the normal way of feeding. And for that reason and many others, breastfeeding doesn't always come naturally to the mother. Sometimes it must be taught.

I hope this book will convince you of the importance of breastfeeding, answer the questions you have and give you the confidence you need to breastfeed successfully. Please keep this book handy, and refer to it after your baby is born.

When choosing how you feed your baby, listen to you heart. Babies are born to be breastfed and your baby has the right to get the very best from you. Give your baby the most precious gifts of all - love, nourishment, and security from your breast. You will both benefit from it!

Some of the sweetest moments of your life will be when you are nursing your baby.

Pamela K. Wiggins, IBCLC

TABLE OF CONTENTS

CHAPTER 1: The Importance of Breastfeeding

Why should I nurse my baby?   1
What are the risks of feeding my baby formula?   4

CHAPTER 2: Preparing to Breastfeed

What can I do to prepare for breastfeeding?   5
Is nipple preparation necessary?   5
Do I have inverted nipples?   6
What can I do if I have flat or inverted nipples?   6

CHAPTER 3: How the Breast Works

How does the breast make milk?   7
What is the letdown?   8
What are foremilk and hindmilk?   8

CHAPTER 4: In the Hospital

How soon after birth should I nurse my baby?   11
When will I have milk?   11
What is rooming-in?   12
What is the best way to hold my baby?   12
How do I get my baby latched on?   14
How do I get the baby off the breast?   15
What are afterpains?   15
Can I nurse twins? How?   16

CHAPTER 5: At Home

How often should I feed my baby?   17
How long should I nurse at each feeding?   18
How can I tell if my baby is getting enough?   18
Should I give water or formula to my baby?   20
Should I try to burp my baby?   20
What is formula?   20
When will my baby sleep through the night?   21
Will I spoil my baby if I pick him up when he cries?   21
Will breastfeeding "tie me down?"   22
Should I use a pacifier?   22
What is a growth spurt?   23
Does my baby have diarrhea?   23
What is a nursing strike?   24
Will my baby bite?   25
How can I keep family members from feeling left out?   25
How can I nurse discreetly or privately in public?   26

CHAPTER 6: Breastfeeding Aids

Do I need to buy any breastfeeding products?   29
Do I need a breast pump?   29
What are breast shells?   30
What is a nipple shield?   30
What are breast pads? Will my breasts leak?   31
Will I need a nursing bra?   31
What is a Supplemental Nursing System (SNS)?   32

CHAPTER 7: Problems the Mother Might Have

What is engorgement?   33
What is a plugged duct? A breast infection?   33
Can I breastfeed if I have a cesarean section?   34
How do I treat sore nipples?   35
Can I nurse if I get sick?   36
Can I still nurse if I am HIV Positive or have AIDS?   36
When will my periods start?   36
Can I get pregnant while nursing?   37
Can I take birth control pills?   37

CHAPTER 8: Problems the Baby Might Have

What is Jaundice? Can I still nurse my baby if he has Jaundice?   39
What is colic? What can I do?   41
Can I breastfeed my premature baby?   42
Is my baby constipated?   42
Can I nurse my sick baby?   42
What is thrush?   43
What is nipple confusion?   43

CHAPTER 9: Diets and Habits

What should I eat while nursing?   45
Are there foods I shouldn't eat?   46
Can I have caffeine drinks?   46
Can I drink alcohol?   46
Can I smoke?   46
Can I take "street" drugs?   47

CHAPTER 10: Beginning Solids and Weaning

When will my baby need solids?   49
How do I begin giving solids?   50
When will my baby wean?   51
Suppose I want to wean? How do I do it?   52

CHAPTER 11: Working and Breastfeeding

Can I work and breastfeed? How?   55
What will I do at work?   56
How do I pump and store milk?   56
What if I have to leave formula?   57
What are my choices?   58
What type of breast pump should I use?   58
How do I hand express my milk?   60

CHAPTER 12: Where to Turn for Help

What is WIC?   63
What is the WIC Peer Counselor Program?   64
What is La Leche League?   64
What is an International Board Certified Lactation Consultant (IBCLC)? 65

More Information:

How To Know If Your Baby is Getting Enough   27
How To Increase Your Milk Supply   28
Hints For Starting Solids   48
Storing Breastmilk   54
When To Ask For Help   62

Index   66
About the Author   69

The Importance of Breastfeeding

Breastfeeding is a mother's gift to herself, her baby and the earth.

Why should I nurse my baby?

• Human breastmilk is the perfect food for your baby. It has all the right ingredients in just the right amounts.

• Breastfeeding will help you bond with your baby. It will help you feel closer to him.

• Mother's milk is easy to digest. Babies seldom get constipated or have diarrhea.

• Breastfed babies are easy to comfort at the breast when they are sick or hurt.

• Breastfed babies have stronger and straighter teeth. They probably won't need braces.

• A mother's milk helps to promote better vision for her baby.

• Because of the special way they suck on the breast, breastfed babies have fewer speech problems.

• Breastmilk helps develop brain cells and can also help increase your baby's IQ.

• Breastfeeding gives your baby the best emotional start. A child who receives security at the breast grows up with self-confidence and trust.

• Breastmilk is always available and at the right temperature. You can feed your baby any time and any place. You will always have food for your baby, even in a disaster.

• Breastfed babies are easy to take wherever you go. There is no need to pack up bottles and formula.

• Breastfed babies smell good. Their dirty diapers don't smell bad and most don't spit up. When they do spit up, it doesn't smell bad and it won't stain clothes.

• Nighttime feedings are easy. Just tuck baby in bed with you to nurse. No warming up bottles in the middle of the night.

• It is cheaper to breastfeed than to bottle feed. Since formula fed babies are sick more often, there are more doctor bills to pay. Working mothers may have to miss more days of work.

• Formula, bottles and liners are expensive. Even if you're on WIC, you won't receive enough formula to completely feed your baby. You will still have to spend money on formula.

• You will feel relaxed and peaceful while you are nursing your baby. A hormone called prolactin is released when the baby is nursing. It helps you to relax and have mothering feelings.

• A breastfed baby always knows who his mother is. Sometimes working mothers worry that their babies will become too attached to the babysitter. Nursing the baby often can help prevent that from happening.

• Breastfeeding can help prevent heavy bleeding following birth. If you decide to formula feed, your uterus will not return to normal as fast.

• Breastfeeding can help you lose the weight you put on during pregnancy.

• Breastfeeding helps to reduce the risk of breast and other female related cancers. It also helps protect children from certain cancers.

• You will get your period back quicker if you formula feed. Breastfeeding usually delays it for several months and you probably won't ovulate until you get your period.

• Making and using formula uses many resources and creates a lot of trash. Breastfeeding avoids this unnecessary waste and doesn't pollute the environment.

• Breastfeeding helps you feel good about yourself because you know you are giving your baby the best. You are also giving of yourself, which is the greatest gift of all.

> *Breastfeeding is a mother's gift to herself, her baby and the earth.*
> – PAMELA K. WIGGINS, IBCLC

What are the risks of feeding my baby formula?

• Formula does not have the special antibodies that help protect your baby from colds, flu, ear infections, and illnesses like asthma, eczema and hay fever. Breastmilk can help protect your baby from all of these.

• Formula fed babies may have more allergies than breastfed babies. Breastfeeding is very important if your family has a history of allergies.

• Formula feeding increases the risks of diabetes in children.

• Formula feeding increases the risk of juvenile rheumatoid arthritis.

• Formula fed babies tend to gain more weight than breastfed babies. Breastfeeding helps protect against obesity.

• Research has also shown that there are more crib deaths (SIDS) among formula fed babies.

• Formula feeding increases the risk of certain childhood cancers.

• Formula feeding increases the risk of heart disease and certain cancers later in life.

Preparing To Breastfeed

Talk to mothers who have successfully breastfed.

What can I do to prepare for breastfeeding?

Even before your baby is born, you can get ready to breastfeed. You should learn all you can about it. There are many good books and videos about breastfeeding. You should also talk to mothers who have **successfully** breastfed, go to a La Leche League meeting or take a breastfeeding class. When you go to the hospital, tell the staff you plan to breastfeed, so they can give you the support you need.

Is nipple preparation necessary?

Not really. The nipples will get tougher as the baby nurses. You don't need to roll or tug at your nipples during pregnancy. That only makes them more tender and removes part of the outer layer of skin. Never use soap or alcohol on the nipples. It will make them too dry. Trying to get colostrum (the first milk) out during pregnancy is not a good idea either. *The key to preventing sore nipples is holding the baby the right way. (See page 12.)*

Do I have inverted nipples?

You can't tell by looking. You need to
do the pinch test. Place your thumb and
fingers about one inch from the nipple (see
picture) and squeeze gently. Most nipples
will stick out. An inverted nipple will go in. If you think that your
nipples are inverted, ask your doctor or midwife about them.

What can I do if I have flat or inverted nipples?

Your breasts and nipples can change during pregnancy.
Hormones may cause your nipples to stick out more by the time
your baby is born. When your baby nurses, he will suck on the
breast, not just on the nipple. As the baby feeds, he will pull the
nipple deeper into his mouth. Even if you do have flat or slightly
inverted nipples, you may be able to gently pull them out with
your fingers (far enough out for your baby to latch on to them).

If your nipples don't stick out far enough, your baby may
need extra help getting started. Ask for help from a lactation
consultant or your WIC counselor. It is very important not to
confuse your baby with bottles or pacifiers. It may be helpful to
use breast shells or nipple shields (chapter 6). With help and a
little time, your baby should be able to nurse.

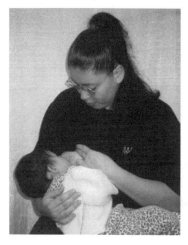

How the Breast Works

The more the baby nurses and removes milk, the more milk you will make.

How does the breast make milk?

When a baby nurses, and gets milk, it causes more milk to be made. That is why it is so important for the mother to nurse often during the first few weeks. The more milk your baby removes, the more the breast makes. It takes about six weeks to build up a good milk supply. Giving your baby bottles of formula will cause you to make less milk.

When the baby is sucking **correctly**, it causes the nerves, located underneath the darker area around the nipple (**areola**,) to tell the brain to release a hormone called **prolactin**. This hormone then signals the milk glands to make milk. Milk is made in the **milk glands** and it travels down the **ducts** and out the **nipple pores** (openings.) Another hormone, **oxytocin**, causes the milk glands to release milk into the ducts.

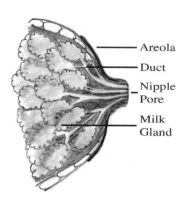

Areola
Duct
Nipple Pore
Milk Gland

What is the letdown?

The **letdown** or **milk ejection reflex** happens when milk is forcefully moved from the milk glands down to the nipple openings. It is caused by a hormone called oxytocin, which is released in the brain when the baby suckles. Oxytocin causes the milk producing cells to release the milk they have made.

Oxytocin is released when the baby sucks. Sometimes it will happen when you hear the baby cry, or if you're just thinking about your baby. Sometimes you will feel a tingling feeling in the breast, or it might begin to leak. Some mothers never feel tingling at all.

It sometimes takes several minutes for the letdown to happen. When you notice your baby swallowing more often, or taking large gulps, you can be sure you have had a letdown. You may have more than one at each feeding.

Sometimes letdowns are so powerful that the milk will come out too fast and the baby will choke or gag. If this happens, take the baby off for a moment before you put the baby back on.

What are foremilk and hindmilk?

Foremilk is the milk baby gets at the beginning of a feeding. It is thin and may look a little blue. It is low in fat and calories. As the baby nurses, foremilk slowly turns to **hindmilk**, which is creamy and higher in fat and calories. Your baby needs plenty of calories in order to grow.

If your baby isn't gaining enough weight, you should nurse longer at each breast so he will get plenty of the higher fat milk. You may also try nursing at only one breast for each feeding. This will help your baby get more of the rich hindmilk.

It is a good idea to let your baby decide when to switch breasts. When he has had enough of the first breast, he may fall asleep, or he may just stop nursing. If he does fall asleep, try waking him.

Then try burping him, and offering him the second breast. He may take it or he may not.

If you switch sides too soon or too often, your baby may get too much foremilk and not enough hindmilk. Sometimes, babies who are getting too much foremilk are fussy and have green, runny stools.

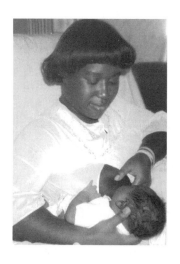

In the Hospital

Put your baby to your breast immediately after birth.

How soon after birth should I nurse my baby?

The sooner you nurse, the better. The ideal time is right after birth. A baby is very alert and calm for the first couple of hours and will usually be able to latch on. Be sure and tell your doctor or midwife ahead of time that you want to nurse as soon as possible.

When will I have milk?

During pregnancy, your breasts will begin to make milk. The first milk you make is called **colostrum**. Sometimes it is yellow and other times it is clear. It is very rich in proteins and it helps protect your baby from getting sick. Colostrum also helps to flush out the baby's digestive system if he has yellow jaundice (page 39). Colostrum turns into mature milk around day 3 or 4. The more you nurse, the quicker your mature milk will come in. Do not wait until it comes in to begin nursing. **It is very important that your baby gets colostrum.**

What is rooming-in?

Most hospitals will allow the baby to stay in the mother's room instead of the nursery. You can begin to bond with your baby and care for his needs. It is also a great way to get breastfeeding off to a good start. If you can't keep your baby with you 24 hours a day, tell the nurse to bring your baby to you for *all* feedings.

What is the best way to hold my baby?

How you hold your newborn is important. When you hold your baby correctly, he should be able to get a mouth full of breast and remove more milk. If he is not positioned just right, he will have a harder time latching on and your nipples could get sore.

There are four basic positions – the *cradle, cross-cradle, football* and *lying down*. You may want to try each of them to see which ones work best for you. If you had a C-section, you can still nurse in any of these positions. You may need extra pillows to help protect your incision.

Breastfeeding should be comfortable for you and your baby. Sit in a comfortable chair and use pillows to support your back and your baby's body. You may want to use a footstool. It is also nice if you have someone help you position your baby.

Cradle Hold

The most popular position is the **cradle hold.** Rest your baby's head on your forearm so his whole body is in a straight line and facing yours. His head should be level with your breast and his back should be supported by your arm. Support your breast with your other hand.

Some mothers like the **cross-cradle hold.** This position can give you more control of the baby's head when he latches on. Start by putting the baby on your lap, facing you. Hold your baby on your forearm and support his head with the heel of your hand on his shoulders. Your other hand should support your breast. After your baby is nursing well in the cross-cradle hold, you can easily switch to the cradle hold by sliding your arm under your baby. You can do this without disturbing him.

Cross-Cradle

If you have a small baby, large breasts or had a C-section, you may prefer to use the **football hold.** Support your baby's head with the heel of your hand at his shoulders. His back will be on your forearm. His head should be level with your breast with his feet behind you. His hands should be on each side of your breast. You may want to support your breast with your other hand. If you are using the football hold while in bed, use extra pillows for support.

Football Hold

Lying down to nurse is a great position. It is comfortable, relaxing and will allow you to get some rest while you are feeding your baby. Place the baby on his side, with his head in line with your breast and bring him in close. Nursing during the night is much easier if you are lying down.

As time goes by, breastfeeding will become easier for you and your baby. You will be able to nurse without thinking about how you are holding him.

Lying Down

How do I get my baby latched on?

No matter how you hold your baby, he must be latched on right.

Rub your baby's nose with your nipple. Wait for him to open WIDE.

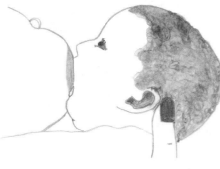

Point your nipple toward the roof of his mouth. Bring him in, chin first. Part of the areola (dark area) should be showing *above* the baby's top lip.

This baby is sucking on the end of the nipple. He is NOT latched on right.

Breastfeeding should NOT hurt. If it hurts, take the baby off and try again. Once you and your baby learn to latch on the right way, breastfeeding will be easy. Good latch-on is the key to successful breastfeeding!

More About Latch On:

When your baby is nursing correctly, your nipple is drawn far into his mouth. His tongue will be well over his bottom gum.

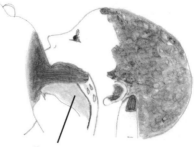

Tongue

• Your baby should be held close and facing you, tummy to tummy (unless he is in the football hold.)

• Your baby's arm should not be between his body and yours.

• His nose should be away from the breast and his chin should be pressed into the breast.

• Both lips should be flanged (poked) out. If his bottom lip is tucked in, pull down on his chin to "untuck" the lip.

How do I get the baby off the breast?

It is better to let the baby come off the breast by himself when he is fully satisfied. If you need to take him off, slide your clean finger into the corner of his mouth until it is between his gums. Keep your finger there until he comes off the breast. Never pull the baby off without doing this, because you might hurt your nipple.

What are afterpains?

In the beginning you might feel some cramping when the baby nurses. This is called afterpains and it means the uterus is getting back to normal. The cramping will go away soon. If it is very painful, take a mild painkiller about half an hour before nursing.

Can I nurse twins? How?

Of course you can nurse twins. Thousands of mothers have nursed twins and even triplets. In fact, breastfeeding twins is easier than preparing two sets of bottles for each feeding. Since many twins are born early, they really need the advantage of mother's milk.

Your breasts will make enough milk for your twins. *Remember, the more you nurse, and the more milk that is removed, the more milk you will make.* Bottles will probably not be necessary for your twins if you are nursing them whenever they need to nurse.

You will want to try different ways of holding your twins if you want to nurse them at the same time. Pillows will help a lot. The football hold works well for some mothers. Just tuck a baby under each arm. Another way is to criss-cross the babies in the cradle hold with your hands or pillows supporting them. The best way is to find the most comfortable way for *you.*

You may want to nurse your twins one at a time. This gives you a chance to bond with each baby individually. You can either give each baby his own breast or switch sides at every feeding. Just make sure that each baby gets enough milk to be satisfied. If you nurse them whenever they are hungry, they will probably gain enough without giving bottles. Keep your babies near your bed at night, so you can nurse without having to get up. You can do it!

At Home

Relax and enjoy being a mother. He won't be a baby for long.

How often should I feed my baby?

You should feed your baby as often as he needs to nurse. Since a newborn's stomach is very small and breastmilk is digested very quickly, your baby should nurse at least 10 times every 24 hours. He should nurse every couple of hours, although at night he may go longer between feedings.

After the first few days, your baby will show signs of hunger when he needs to nurse. Don't put your baby on a schedule, just watch him. He may put his hand in his mouth or lick his lips. He may also squirm or turn his head like he is looking for the breast. Don't wait until your baby starts to cry before you feed him, it will be harder for him to latch on.

If your baby sleeps more than four hours during the day, you will need to wake him up to nurse. Here are some ways to wake a sleeping baby:

• Change his diaper.

• Remove blankets or extra clothing.

• Put him skin to skin.

• Pat his face, arms and legs with a damp washcloth.

Your baby might fall asleep before he gets
enough. If he does, try to wake him up
by burping him or patting him. But, if
you can't wake him, don't worry. He will
probably wake up by himself in a few
minutes and then nurse until he gets
enough.

Some babies "cluster feed." They may go
longer between feedings during the day and
then in the evening seem to want to nurse all
the time. This is common for a lot of babies in the early weeks.
When a baby cries, he has a need. It may be that he is hot, cold,
wet, hungry or just lonely. If he can't be comforted any other
way than nursing, then he needs to nurse. You can't over-feed
a breastfed baby. He will stop when he has enough. Be patient
during the early days. As your milk supply builds up and his
tummy gets bigger, he will nurse less often.

How long should I nurse at each feeding?

At the beginning of each feeding, your milk is thin and low in
calories. As your baby nurses, the milk will become creamy and
higher in fat. Your baby needs plenty of calories in order to grow.
You should nurse your baby on one breast for 20 to 30 minutes
or until he comes off by himself.

You can then try offering him the other side. If he doesn't want
to nurse, start on the second breast next time. At the end of a
feeding, your breast should feel softer and lighter. You may also
see milk pooling in his mouth.

How can I tell if my baby is getting enough breastmilk?

If your baby is content, alert, nursing at least 10 times every
24 hours and gaining weight, he is probably getting enough
breastmilk. It's normal for babies to lose a few ounces the first
few days, but they should regain their birthweight by 2 weeks.

Counting your baby's diapers is one way to know if he is getting enough breastmilk. Your baby should have 1 or 2 wet diapers the first day and each day he should be wetting more diapers. By the end of the first week, he should be having at least 6 wet diapers a day. The urine should have little or no color. Also, by the end of the first week, he should be having at least one or two large bowel movements or several small ones a day. By then, your baby's stool should have turned from blackish brown to yellow.

There are other ways to tell. When your baby nurses, you should be able to see his jaws moving in a steady rhythm and you hear or see him swallowing milk after every 2-3 sucks. Your breasts will seem softer and lighter at the end of a feed and you will see milk pooling in your baby's mouth when he comes off the breast.

Remember, that the more your baby nurses and removes milk, the more milk you will make. So nursing often means you will have plenty of milk for your baby.

If you are worried that your baby is not getting enough, watch for these signs of dehydration:

• he acts limp or sick
• he has dark yellow urine
• his mouth and lips are dry or
• the soft spot on the top of his head sinks in.

Dehydration is serious. If you think your baby is dehydrated, take him to the doctor right away.

Should I give water or formula to my baby?

Breastmilk has everything your baby needs. You and your baby get the most benefits from breastfeeding when the baby is getting breastmilk only. Using formula reduces the benefits of breastfeeding. You might worry that you don't have enough milk for your baby. *Remember that the more you nurse, and the more milk is removed, the more milk you will make.* If you fill the baby up with formula or water, he will nurse less and you won't make as much milk. Water is not needed for a completely breastfed baby.

Should I try to burp my baby?

Breastfed babies don't swallow as much air as bottle babies. However, you should try to burp the baby after he has finished the first breast. If he hasn't burped in a minute or two, he probably doesn't have to.

Sometimes when a baby is not burped during a feeding, he may feel full and fall asleep too soon. This could affect your milk supply and the baby's weight. Burping him will usually help him to take more milk. This is something that dad can do to also feel close to the baby.

What is formula?

Formula is made from cow's milk or soybeans. It has ingredients added to it and ingredients taken out to make it more like human milk. But, there are still many differences. Scientists will never be able to make anything like human breastmilk. The main difference is the special antibodies that are in *your* breastmilk. These antibodies help keep your baby from getting sick.

Formulas are not as easy to digest as human milk. Cow's milk formulas form large curds in the baby's stomach and may cause constipation. Some babies can be allergic to cow's milk formula.

If that happens, he will probably be given soybean formula. Remember that no formulas are as good for your baby as your own breastmilk.

When will my baby sleep through the night?

All babies are different. While some babies may never sleep through the night, others start to sleep through at two weeks. A lot of bottle fed babies don't sleep all night either.

Breastfed babies need to nurse during the night for the first few weeks. Since breastmilk is digested so quickly, they need to be fed often. Nursing during the night also helps build up your milk supply.

Some babies sleep through the night for a while, and then when they start teething, they start waking again. When they are in pain, they can't sleep, and nursing will probably help them get back to sleep.

Babies who wake up and cry during the night have a need. They may be hungry or wet, or they might just need to be near the mother. Many breastfeeding mothers keep the baby's crib nearby so they can pick up the baby and nurse without ever getting up.

Some moms feed cereal or formula at bedtime, but is is not a good idea. Your baby may not be able to handle it, or he may be allergic to it. This could cause more problems than waking up during the night.

Don't worry if your baby is not sleeping through the night yet. *He will eventually sleep all night.*

Will I spoil my baby if I pick him up when he cries?

When a baby cries, he has a need. He may be hungry, wet, need burping, or just need to be held. Emotional needs are just as important as physical needs, and crying is the only way your baby has to let you know he has a need.

Your baby wants and needs to feel you close by, and if he stops crying when you pick him up and cuddle him, then that is what he needs. There are some babies who may need to be held most of the time.

You may find that using a carrier or a sling can help. The baby is able to stay close while you are doing other things. The baby feels very secure and cries much less. Many fathers also enjoy wearing their babies!

You can't *spoil* a newborn baby. And if you don't meet his needs while he is a baby, he might have more serious emotional problems later.

A baby who is cared for and loved will learn to love and trust his parents. The well-loved child will grow up to trust others. He will feel secure and be able to adjust to life's problems. Breastfeeding is the natural way to meet all your baby's needs.

Will breastfeeding tie me down?

It is true that breastfed babies have to be fed more often than bottle fed babies, and they can't be left for long periods of time. Some mothers may feel a little tied down. After the first few weeks you will have a good milk supply and you can leave your baby once in a while. He can learn to take a bottle of breastmilk from a babysitter. If you are shy about nursing in public, learning to nurse discreetly can help (page 26). If you have to go back to work, you can still breastfeed (chapter 11).

Should I use a pacifier?

While a pacifier may be useful at times, it can affect your milk supply. It is best not to get in the habit of using it all the time.

If you are somewhere where you can't nurse, then you may use a pacifier temporarily. Holding the baby when he is sucking a pacifier is better than putting him to bed with it.

If your baby is given a pacifier every time he fusses, he may not nurse enough to keep up your milk supply, and he may not gain weight as he should. Your milk supply will clearly be affected if you use a pacifier too often.

Remember, babies can have all their sucking needs met at the breast. Making your baby peaceful and comfortable is part of breastfeeding.

What is a growth spurt?

Most babies go through periods of sudden growth during the early months. They may want to nurse more often during these times. Growth spurts only last a day or two, just long enough for the baby to build up your milk supply to meet his growing needs. Knowing about growth spurts will help you when the time comes.

The first growth spurt should come around the 10th to 14th day. This is also about the time you notice that your breasts don't seem as full as they did at first. This is normal, so don't think you have lost your milk. The baby is just making sure you make even more.

The second growth spurt comes around 4 to 6 weeks. The baby is now growing at a faster rate. Just nurse often for a day or two, and soon the baby will return to his normal feeding pattern.

Does my baby have diarrhea?

The bowel movements (BM) of a breastfed baby are quite different than a baby who is formula fed. They are loose, and soft and don't smell bad. The color is usually light yellow and may look a lot like mustard.

While some mothers may think that this is diarrhea, it is not. When a baby has diarrhea, the stool is thin and watery.

Your baby may have a little BM after every feeding, or have 1 or 2 big ones a day. Both are normal. Because breastmilk is so well digested, a completely breastfed baby should not become constipated.

What is a nursing strike?

Between the age of 4 and 8 months, a baby may suddenly refuse to nurse. It could be that he is teething and it hurts his gums to nurse, or he could have an ear infection, sore throat, or cold. Sometimes there is no apparent reason. Whatever the reason, you must try to keep up your milk supply by pumping about every 3-4 hours. And you must continue to gently offer the breast to him. Meanwhile you have to find some other way of feeding your baby.

You can try feeding him your expressed (pumped) milk with a cup or spoon or medicine dropper. Using a bottle can make it even harder to get him back on the breast. He might quickly realize he doesn't have to work as hard to get milk from a bottle as he does from the breast. In fact, using a bottle could have caused the nursing strike in the first place.

It may take several days for the baby to start back nursing, and during this time you will need to give him lots of skin to skin contact and cuddling. You can even try nursing him while he is asleep. Some babies will nurse while asleep even while *on strike*.

Don't confuse a nursing strike with weaning. Weaning occurs gradually, and strikes happen suddenly. Although this will be a very trying time, hang in there. Keep offering the breast but don't try to force him. Soon he should be back to normal.

Will my baby bite?

While many babies never bite, some do. Sometimes a baby will bite when he is teething. His gums are sore and when he nurses, they hurt more. A baby might also bite if you try to nurse him when he isn't hungry or at the end of a feeding when he has had enough.

It is impossible for a baby to bite and nurse at the same time because the baby's tongue is between the bottom teeth and your nipple. Only when he has stopped nursing, will he be able to bite. Watch your baby. When he stops sucking or swallowing, break the suction and take him off the breast before he starts to bite.

If he does bite, gently take him off the breast and firmly say "no." After two or three times, most babies will know that they must not bite. You do not have to wean the baby when he gets teeth.

How can I keep family members from feeling left out?

Unfortunately, some family members may not understand the advantages of breastfeeding. They might be afraid it will be embarrassing if you nurse in front of them. They may even feel left out.

If your loved ones are not supportive, try explaining why you chose to breastfeed. Invite them to read this book, take a breastfeeding class or introduce them to other breastfeeding mothers.

When you learn to nurse discreetly, you can nurse in the same room with your family members without anyone being embarrassed. Nursing in the same room will also keep you from feeling isolated.

There are many ways you can include family members. They can bathe your baby, change his diapers, play with him, rock him to sleep or help with other household chores. Daddies don't feel as left out if they sit down with mom and baby while they are nursing.

Most family members are quickly won over when they see how well babies get along on breastmilk. Don't let anyone keep you from giving your baby the very best.

How can I nurse discreetly or privately in public?

Your baby will need to nurse no matter where you are, what you're doing or who is around. If you learn to nurse discreetly you can feed him without being afraid that people will see your breast. What you wear makes a big difference.

While there are clothes made especially for nursing moms, you can also use clothes you already have. It is hard to be discreet if you lift your breast out through the neck of a shirt. It's easier to lift up your shirt from the bottom and tuck the baby in.

Most mothers find that wearing layers works best. For example, you can wear an unbuttoned shirt or jacket over a shirt. The outer layer will cover your breast from the side.

If you wear a button up shirt by itself, be sure to unbutton from the bottom instead of the top. Wearing a skirt and top instead of a dress, makes nursing easier for dress up occasions. You can also use a blanket to cover your baby while he is nursing.

You have the right to feed your baby whenever he is hungry. Most states have laws to protect nursing mothers.

It takes a little practice to learn to nurse discreetly, but soon you will be nursing anywhere and everywhere and no one will even know.

HOW TO KNOW IF YOUR BABY IS GETTING ENOUGH:

- He is nursing at least 10-12 times in 24 hours.

- He is content, alert, and gaining weight.

- You see his jaws moving in a steady rhythm and he is swallowing every 2-3 sucks.

- You see milk pooling in your baby's mouth when he comes off the breast.

- Your breasts feel softer and lighter at the end of each feeding.

- Counting your baby's diapers can also help you know if he is getting enough.

(See pages 18-19 for more information.)

HOW TO INCREASE YOUR MILK SUPPLY

- Let your baby nurse whenever he wants to.
- Drink plenty of fluids.
- Eat nutritious food.
- Get plenty of rest.
- Give lots of skin-to-skin contact.
- Nurse for at least 30 minutes at each breast.
- If you are using formula, cut back gradually.
- Don't use a pacifier.

6

Breastfeeding Aids

To breastfeed, all you need is your baby!

Do I need to buy any breastfeeding products?

There are many products marketed to breastfeeding moms. While some of them may be nice to have, none of them are necessary to breastfeed successfully. To breastfeed, all you need is your baby! Remember that women have been breastfeeding since the beginning of time without any of these things. Keep things simple. Having too much baby stuff around will only complicate your life. Focus on your baby, not things.

Do I need a breast pump?

You may want a breast pump if you will be separated from your baby, and still want to feed him breastmilk. Many mothers use a breast pump when they go back to work or leave the baby for a few hours. You may also want a pump if you or your baby have to stay in the hospital.

While a breast pump is convenient to have, they are not necessary. The best way to collect milk from the breast is to express it by hand. The types of breast pumps and hand expression are discussed in detail in chapter 11.

What are breast shells?

Breast shells are made of hard plastic and fit in the bra. They are used to keep sore nipples dry and from rubbing against clothing while they are healing. They are also used by women who have inverted nipples. They work by putting a gentle pressure on the base of the nipple and training it to stand out. You can get them from most La Leche League leaders, lactation consultants or maternity shops.

What is a nipple shield?

A nipple shield is made of very soft, thin silicone that fits over your nipple while nursing. It has holes in it like a bottle nipple. Nipple shields can be used for sore or cracked nipples, engorged breasts or for inverted or flat nipples. They can also be helpful if the baby has trouble latching on, has a very weak suck or to help preemies to latch on. Many of these problems can be overcome in time, with the help of a lactation consultant.

Some people believe that nipple shields interfere with milk production, but research has never really proved it. If you have been given a nipple shield because of flat nipples, inverted nipples or a latch-on problem, and you want to get your baby off of it, you might try letting him start nursing with it in place and removing it when the nipple has been drawn out enough for him to latch on.

Remember, most babies with latch-on problems or very weak sucks can be trained to suck correctly with time and patience and the help of a lactation consultant. A nipple shield may seem to solve the problem, but ideally, the baby should be able to nurse without it.

Sometimes, a baby will just not be able to latch on any other way than using a nipple shield. If it comes down to a choice of formula feeding or using a nipple shield to nurse, then use the shield. Just be sure to weigh your baby often to make sure he is getting enough breastmilk. You can continue trying to get him to nurse without it. Most babies just outgrow the need for it after a little while.

What are breast pads? Will my breasts leak?

Breast pads are put into the bra to absorb any milk that may leak if you have a **letdown** between feedings. In the early weeks, while you are building up your milk supply, you may leak. This can happen when you are away from home and thinking of your baby, or even when you hear another baby cry. Some mothers have a lot of leaking and others may never leak at all. Sometimes a mother will leak with her first baby but not with the second. Most of the time, leaking goes away in a few weeks.

If you do start to leak, just press your arms against your breasts, and that will usually stop it. Leaking is not as noticeable if you are wearing a dark print shirt.

Will I need a nursing bra?

Nursing bras are designed to make breastfeeding easier. They are sold in many stores and catalogs in many sizes, fabrics and styles. Most have flaps that can be unhooked to expose the nipple. Others are made of stretch fabric that can be pulled away from the nipple.

While nursing bras may be nice to have, they are not necessary to breastfeed. In fact, many mothers just use a regular bra. Even though most mothers like to wear a bra for support, some moms are comfortable without wearing any kind of bra (especially if you are at home). Either way, it is up to you.

What is a Supplemental Nursing System (SNS)?

This breastfeeding aid consists of a small bottle (worn around the neck) and a length of very small tubing, which carries breastmilk or formula to the mother's nipple. The baby sucks on the end of the tube and the mother's breast at the same time.

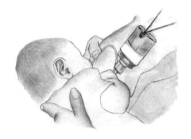

If a baby is having latch-on problems it can help train him to nurse. It also stimulates the breasts to produce milk. An SNS can be useful when a mother wants to get her milk supply back, when the baby is nipple confused, or when an adoptive mother wants to feed at the breast.

Problems the Mother Might Have

Proper latch-on and nursing often will prevent most problems.

What is engorgement?

Breastmilk usually comes in by the fourth day. It's normal for breasts to feel hot, swollen and heavy, but this should only last about 24 hours. If, after 24 hours, your breasts are still swollen, hard or painful you may be engorged.

The key to preventing and relieving engorgement is to nurse often. If nursing doesn't relieve the fullness, use a breast pump or hand express your milk. Before you nurse or express your milk, take a warm shower or use warm wet cloths on your breasts to help the milk flow. When you are done, ice packs may help reduce swelling. Take a mild painkiller if you need it.

Sometimes a breast is so swollen that the nipple flattens out and the baby can't get latched on. If this happens, squeeze or pump out a little milk right before your baby nurses to make your nipple stick out. If you nurse often, you should feel better soon.

What is a plugged duct? A breast infection?

A plugged duct is a small tender spot caused by a duct that is stopped up with milk. It might happen when the baby decides to sleep through the night, or if you get busy and don't nurse as often. Sometimes a tight bra can be pressing on a milk duct. Stress and poor eating habits can also cause plugged milk ducts. Here are some things you can do if you have a plugged duct:

- Get lots of rest and nurse *often*. Take the baby to bed with you.

- Apply a hot, wet washcloth to the breast, soak the breast in warm water, or take a hot shower or bath.

- Massage the breast before nursing to help the milk flow.

- Hold the baby so his chin points toward the spot that hurts.

- Change the way you hold him each time you nurse so all ducts will be emptied.

If you have the same symptoms *plus* feel achy like you have the flu and a fever, you probably have a **breast infection (mastitis)**. You get a breast infection if you do not treat a plugged duct. If your breast does get infected, you should use the same treatments as above and also call the doctor. He will probably prescribe an antibiotic for you. Remember to keep nursing often. The milk from an infected breast will not harm the baby. Breast infections are common during holidays because a lot of mothers get so busy they skip feedings.

Can I breastfeed if I have a cesarean section?

Yes, you can breastfeed if you have had a C-section. Don't let it stop you from giving the best to your baby. Your baby may be too sleepy to nurse because of the medications you had during surgery and you might need to ask for help from your nurse for the first few feedings. Ask her to show you how to hold the baby and for extra pillows to protect your incision. It may be more comfortable to nurse lying down at first. Having someone to help you out at home for a few days is a good idea, too. Many mothers feel that breastfeeding after a C-section helps make up for not having a more natural childbirth.

How do I treat sore nipples?

In the beginning, it is common to have slightly sore nipples, but if the baby is held in the right way, your nipples should never blister, crack or bleed. Remember to get as much of the areola (darker area) in the baby's mouth as you can (page 14). His body should be facing you and more of the darker area around the nipple should be showing above the nipple than below. His chin should be pressed into the breast and both lips should be flanged (poked) out. Take your finger and pull down on his chin if his bottom lip is tucked in. If your nipples do get sore, you should do the following:

• Change the way you hold him at each feeding. This puts the pressure of his gums on a different spot each time. (cradle hold, lying down and football hold)

• Nurse more often, but for shorter lengths of time. If you go longer between feedings, the baby will be hungrier and nurse too hard and make them even more sore.

• Rub breastmilk on the nipple after each feeding and let dry. It can help heal them.

• Don't use soap or alcohol on your nipples.

• If the pain is severe, take a mild painkiller about 30 minutes before nursing.

If your nipples are *cracked or bleeding*, rub a small amount of 100% medical grade lanolin on your nipples. It will help the wound to heal much faster and won't form a scab. Medical grade lanolin does not have to be removed before the baby nurses. It is available in large discount stores or it may be available from your WIC breastfeeding counselor.

Can I nurse if I get sick?

Unless you are very, very sick, you should continue nursing. Your baby probably won't catch what you have. In fact, before you even come down with any symptoms, your body has already produced antibodies in your milk, which will help keep your baby from getting what you have.

If you are sick enough to need medicine, make sure your doctor knows you are breastfeeding so he can prescribe medicine that won't harm your baby. Most antibiotics and over the counter medication can be taken while breastfeeding.

The benefits of breastfeeding usually outweigh the risks of your baby getting a serious disease from you. If you do have a serious disease, talk with your doctor.

Can I nurse if I am HIV Positive or have AIDS?

The AIDS virus *can* be passed through breastmilk. Before any *pregnant woman at risk* decides to nurse, she should be tested for HIV infection. You are at risk if you have had unprotected sex with more than one partner, if your partner has had unprotected sex with someone else, or if you have shared needles during drug use. Most public health agencies recommend that HIV+ women do not nurse.

When will my periods start?

Most mothers who are nursing completely (no solids, water, or formula) will not have menstrual periods for several months. Some women may even go much longer than that. It depends on your hormones. Nursing while you are having a period will not affect your milk and is not a reason to wean. However, your nipples and breasts might be tender during this time.

Can I get pregnant while nursing?

Yes, you can get pregnant while breastfeeding, but it is rare to ovulate before you have your first menstrual period. Complete breastfeeding (no solids, formula, or even pacifiers) may protect you for the first 4 or 5 months. If it is important that you don't get pregnant, use some other type of birth control. Ask your doctor for advice on birth control.

Can I take birth control pills?

Like all other medication, you should consult with your doctor about birth control options. It is best to avoid any type of medications that contain estrogen, which will affect your milk supply. Even the low dose or mini pill (progestin only) may affect the milk supply in some women. There are safer forms of birth control for nursing mothers.

8

Problems the Baby Might Have

Even if your baby has problems, breastfeeding is still best.

What is Jaundice? Can I still nurse my baby if he has Jaundice?

Jaundice happens when the baby can't get rid of **bilirubin**, the by-product of extra red blood cells that have built up in the womb. It may be scary to hear your baby has (yellow) jaundice, but it is usually nothing to worry about. You can continue to breastfeed. In fact, nursing often is the best thing you can do.

If your doctor thinks your baby has jaundice, he will measure the bilirubin level. If you had a healthy, full-term baby and the level is below 20 mg/dl (and rising slowly), it is probably **not** serious. Your doctor should still keep a close eye on it.

The baby gets rid of most of the excess bilirubin by having bowel movements (BMs). Colostrum (your first milk) acts as a laxative so you should nurse often so that he will have more BMs. The more he has, the quicker the jaundice will go away.

Don't take the baby off the breast and give him formula, because it could constipate him and make the problem worse. You can't "flush out" bilirubin with water either, most bilirubin is passed in bowel movements, not urine. Normal physiologic jaundice (early-onset jaundice) starts about the second or third day and gradually disappears in a week or so. Almost all babies have some degree of this type of jaundice. It is nothing to worry about.

Jaundice that appears during the second week (late-onset jaundice or breastmilk jaundice) and continues for several weeks is thought to be another form of physiologic jaundice. Some experts think that it may be caused by something in the mother's blood that causes bilirubin to be reabsorbed. This type of jaundice is not harmful either, but the doctor may want to take the baby off the breast for a day or two and feed him formula until the bilirubin count goes down. Many experts think giving formula is not necessary because jaundice will go away on its own.

Pathological jaundice is more serious and can be caused by disease, infections, drugs or blood problems. This type of jaundice shows up within the first 24 hours. Your doctor will find out the cause and treat it. It is not necessary to stop breastfeeding.

If the bilirubin count starts to rise quickly, jaundiced babies are sometimes treated with special lights that help break down the bilirubin that's stored in the skin. The lights will not hurt your baby and he won't have to stay under them all the time. Nursing your baby a lot during this time is the best thing **you** can do for him. Sometimes jaundiced babies are very sleepy. It is still important to feed him often, even if he doesn't act hungry.

Instead of special lights, you can also place your baby near a window during the day. Daylight helps lower the level of bilirubin. Keep the room warm and dress your baby only in a diaper so the light can reach him. Just don't put him in direct sunlight because he could get overheated or the light might hurt his eyes.

> *If your baby's skin and eyes start to look yellow after you get home, call your doctor.*

What is colic? What can I do?

When your baby cries hard and loud for long periods of time every day, he might have colic. Your baby will seem to be in terrible pain and nothing you do will seem to help. The screaming usually lasts 2 or 3 hours at night. No one knows for sure, but it is probably caused by an immature nervous or digestive system. Thankfully, by the third month most colic goes away.

Rest assured that breastfeeding is the best thing you can do for a colicky baby. He would probably feel much worse if he were bottle fed. It is much easier for him to digest breastmilk than formula. Nursing will also help soothe him.

Your colicky baby will want to nurse often and for long periods of time, but be careful because sometimes he will get too much milk and his tummy will hurt even more. To keep him from getting too much: try nursing every 2 hours, give him only one breast at a time and burp him often. A pacifier may also be helpful between feedings.

A colicky baby will need lots of skin-to-skin contact and soft, calm handling. Other things that can help are to give him a warm bath, swaddle him in a blanket, hold, rock, or walk him. Dad can help with these things, too. Mylecon drops might help too. You can get them at the drug store.

Sometimes colic is caused by an allergy to something in your diet. Milk and dairy products are often the cause. If your baby has colic, try cutting out all milk and dairy products for a few days to see if the colic goes away. After a few weeks, the baby may be able to handle it and you can slowly start drinking milk. *You do not have to drink milk to make milk*. You can get your calcium from green leafy vegetables or even calcium tablets. Caffeine drinks can also cause colic symptoms. Cut back on these if your baby has colic.

Can I breastfeed my premature baby?

Breastmilk is the best food for all babies. Preemies do much better if they are fed breastmilk. Your milk is perfect for your baby. It is high in protein and other important nutrients. It is easier to digest than any formula and causes less stress on the baby.

While your baby is in the hospital, you will probably be encouraged to pump (or hand express) your milk for him. As he gets stronger, you should be able to feed him directly from your breast. Pumping will help sustain your milk supply until this happens.

Your preemie may have difficulty nursing at first, but with time and patience he will eventually be able to latch on and nurse. A lactation consultant or a trained nurse can help you make the transition from pumping to nursing.

Pumping may seem difficult, but you will feel better knowing you are giving your baby something no one else can.

Is my baby constipated?

Completely breastfed babies (no formula or solids) should not get constipated. But, after the first few weeks, it is normal for a breastfed baby to go several days without a bowel movement. Don't worry. He is not constipated. The stool will still be loose and runny. When a baby (who is getting formula or other food) gets constipated, the BMs are hard and dry.

Can I nurse my sick baby?

If your baby gets sick, it is almost always better to keep nursing. Since breastmilk is so easy to digest, it is sometimes the only food a sick baby can handle. Sick babies usually want to nurse more often. It helps comfort them.

What is thrush?

Thrush is a yeast infection in the baby's mouth. It looks like white patches on his tongue, gums and inside his cheeks. It may also show up as a diaper rash that peels or looks like red dots. It is often caused by antibiotics that have been given to either the mother or the baby.

When a baby has thrush, it will usually spread to the mother's nipples and they may become red and very sore. When you get sore nipples, after several weeks or even months of breastfeeding, look for signs of thrush in the baby.

The treatment for thrush usually involves nystatin (Mycostatin) ointment or drops. Both the baby's mouth and the mother's nipples have to be treated with it. See page 35 for treatment of sore nipples.

What is nipple confusion?

Sucking on an artificial nipple is different than sucking on the mother's breast, and many babies get confused after only a few bottles or pacifiers. They actually seem to forget how to nurse. It is harder for the baby to nurse than to bottle feed. He has to move his jaws and his tongue a certain way to get milk. With a bottle, all he has to do is create a suction and swallow.

If your baby has become nipple confused, he can be re-taught to breastfeed. Keep trying and take away all bottles and pacifiers. If he won't nurse at all, pump your breasts and feed him breastmilk with an eyedropper, spoon, or cup. Most of the time, after a couple of days, he will get back on the breast. But if he doesn't, don't give up. Ask for help from your lactation consultant or WIC breastfeeding counselor.

9
Diet & Habits

Most mothers can eat anything they want while breastfeeding.

What should I eat while nursing?

You should eat a good healthy diet just like you did during pregnancy. Healthy foods include whole grains, cereal, beans, rice and pasta and, of course, fruits and vegetables. Also eat meat, fish, eggs, milk and cheese. Learn to read labels and don't eat foods with a lot of added chemicals. You may need to eat about 400-500 more calories a day. Just make sure those extra calories are good for you, not junk food!

You do not have to drink large amounts to breastfeed. Just drink when you are thirsty. Water and natural fruit juices are better for you than soft drinks.

It is not a good idea to go on any kind of reducing diet while breastfeeding. Breastfeeding will help you gradually lose the weight you gained during pregnancy. For more advice on healthy eating habits, ask your doctor or WIC nutritionist.

Are there foods I shouldn't eat?

Most nursing mothers can eat anything they want to. Once in a while, very young babies can't handle really spicy foods or gas producing foods like cabbage, broccoli or beans. They **might** make your baby fussy. Large amounts of chocolate or caffeine may also upset him. Try eating different foods, a little at a time, to see how your baby reacts to them. If something really makes him fussy, don't eat it for a couple of weeks. As he grows, he can handle different foods in your diet.

Can I have caffeine drinks?

Coffee, tea, and soft drinks with caffeine should be limited. Caffeine does pass through the milk and makes some babies restless and fussy. You can try decaffeinated coffee, herbal tea and caffeine-free soft drinks. Water is better for you than soft drinks.

Can I drink alcohol?

Alcohol is a drug and it *does* pass through the milk to your baby. Nursing babies whose mothers are heavy drinkers sometimes don't gain enough weight and their central nervous systems are affected. Alcohol also affects your letdown. If you do choose to drink alcohol, don't do it often, and do it *soon after* you nurse, not right before.

Can I smoke?

Heavy smoking can cause you to make less milk, and the milk will have lower levels of vitamin C. Your baby will also have more coughs and colds. If you must smoke, please don't smoke near your baby and don't let other people smoke around your baby. The nicotine levels in the milk will be lower if you smoke after nursing instead of just before. If you do smoke, and just can't quit, it is very important that you breastfeed. It will help protect your baby from getting sick so often.

Can I take recreational drugs?

Recreational drugs should **not** be used while breastfeeding. Marijuana, heroin, cocaine and other similar drugs will hurt **you and your baby.**

HINTS FOR STARTING SOLIDS

• Don't be in a hurry to start solids. Wait until your baby is about 6 months old.

• Start slowly. Offer only one or two feedings a day.

• Always offer just one food at a time.

• A teaspoon or two per feeding is enough to start.

• Don't force your baby to eat.

• Start with rice cereal or oatmeal. Mix with breastmilk.

• Add mashed fruits and vegetables gradually.

• Add mashed meats last.

• Don't feed cow milk or eggs until your baby is at least a year old.

• Mash table food your family eats instead of buying expensive baby food.

10
Beginning Solids & Weaning

Breastmilk is all a baby needs for the first 6 months.

When will my baby need solids?

Your milk has everything your baby needs for about the first six months. After this he may need some iron-rich foods in addition to breastmilk. There is no other food that is as good for your baby as breastmilk and the more solids he eats, the less he will nurse. When you start feeding solids, your breasts will make less milk.

Here are signs your baby is ready for solids:

• He may start asking to nurse more often and just won't seem satisfied. This could mean that he is ready for solids, or it could be for some other reason, like teething.

• He will be able to move food to the back of his mouth and swallow it, instead of pushing it out with his tongue.

• He will be getting teeth.

• He will be able to sit up by himself.

• He will start reaching for or "asking" for your food.

• He will be able to hold food in his hands and put it in his mouth.

All of these signs tell you that your baby is ready for solid food, but don't rush him. Make sure he is really ready for solids before offering them.

How do I begin giving solids?

First of all, nurse first. Nursing first will help maintain your milk supply.

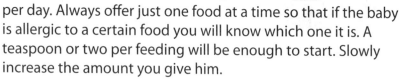

Solids should be started very slowly with just one or two feedings per day. Always offer just one food at a time so that if the baby is allergic to a certain food you will know which one it is. A teaspoon or two per feeding will be enough to start. Slowly increase the amount you give him.

Never force your baby to eat. If your baby refuses a certain food one day, try again in a week or so. Forcing food could make him overweight.

If your baby is allergic to a certain food, he might be fussy, have a rash on his bottom, have cold symptoms, ear infections or stomach upsets.

It is generally recommended that you start solids by offering rice cereal or oatmeal. After you are sure he can handle this, offer him strained fruits and vegetables. At six or seven months, you may give him strained meat, chicken or fish.

Juice may be given in a cup. Cow milk or whole eggs should not be given until the baby is over a year old. When the baby is over a year old, he should be able to chew bite size pieces of food and his need for breastmilk will decrease.

You do not have to buy baby food. A small food grinder or even a fork can mash most table food. Adding a little juice or breastmilk to food will make it thinner. By making your own baby food, you will get the baby used to what the rest of your family eats and save money also. Homemade foods are better for your baby than store-bought baby foods because they don't have as much salt, sugar and fillers.

Ask your doctor or WIC nutritionist for more information on what to feed your baby. Just remember, for the first few months, there is *nothing* you can give your baby that is as good for him as breastmilk.

When will my baby wean?

The American Academy of Pediatrics recommends that you breastfeed for at least a year. They also recommend no formula, juice or other foods for the first six months. When the baby is six months old, he may be ready for solids, but breastmilk will still be important. It will continue to provide antibodies that will keep him from getting sick.

As soon as you start giving your baby solids, you are beginning to wean. Many babies completely wean sometime before their second birthday. If you want to wean your baby before he weans himself, do so very gradually and with love.

If the baby is allowed to wean himself (baby-led weaning) he will usually wean sometime during the second year. However, since all babies are different, they wean at different times. Some babies wean at nine months and others wean at three years.

Don't worry if your baby wants to nurse past his second birthday. This is normal for many babies and there is nothing wrong with it.

Older babies who nurse get their main nourishment from solid foods, but breastmilk is still very important for them. It still keeps them from getting as sick, and satisfies emotional and sucking needs. Nursing is very helpful when the baby is sick or hurt or afraid.

Studies have shown that nursing a toddler does not make him too dependent on the mother. In fact, children who are nursed for a long time usually grow up to be independent and self reliant.

A good rule to remember when the baby is weaning: Never offer the breast, but don't refuse it when he wants it.

Suppose I want to wean? How do I do it?

When you are the one who wants to begin weaning (mother-led weaning), you must plan to do so very slowly so the baby will not feel rejected. Weaning slowly is better for you too. If you wean too quickly, you might become engorged and get a breast infection.

If the baby is under a year old, you will need to wean him to a bottle because he will still have strong sucking needs. Some mothers wait a little longer and wean to a cup.

Begin by doing away with one feeding every few days. Start with the feeding he least enjoys. You will have to replace it with formula, juice or a snack at this time. Then after a few days, when he seems satisfied with the replacement, drop another feeding. Keep on like this until he is no longer breastfeeding.

Your pediatrician or WIC counselor can recommend which formula to feed your baby. Do not feed your baby regular cow milk if he is under a year old because it is so hard to digest and may cause allergies.

During the time you are trying to wean your baby, give him lots of extra cuddling and loving. You may find that it is really hard for him to give up nursing at bedtime. If nursing him for a few minutes at night helps get him to sleep in peace, why not let him? Someday your baby will grow up, and you will miss that special time you spent with him!

STORING BREASTMILK
It is safe to store FRESH breastmilk:

- 8 hours at room temperature (Discard if not used that day.)
- 5 days in the refrigerator
- 2 weeks in the freezer section of a one-door refrigerator
- 3 months in the freezer section of a two-door refrigerator
- 6-12 months in a 0 degree deep-freeze

Important: Milk that has been thawed in the refrigerator should be used within 24 hours. Milk that has been thawed on the counter or under running water should be used within 4 hours. Do not refreeze breastmilk.

11

Working & Breastfeeding

Stay home with your baby as long as you can. You will not regret it.

Can I work and breastfeed? How?

There are many women who have no choice about working. They simply have to work to make ends meet. But they can still breastfeed. In fact, more and more mothers are doing just that. And many mothers say that breastfeeding helps make up for the time spent away from the baby. These mothers are also grateful that their babies won't be catching every little infection going around in the day care center. Breastfeeding and working takes commitment, but it is well worth it. It is better to wait until the baby is at least six weeks old before going back to work, and the longer you can put it off, the better. Talk with your employer and see if you can take longer off.

When you do go back to work, you will have to put the baby on a schedule. Your day will probably go like this:

• Get up a little earlier, so you will have plenty of time to nurse before leaving home.

• The babysitter may have to give a bottle at least every 3 hours. (Breastmilk is best, but you can leave formula if you have to.)

• Nurse the baby as soon as possible after work and when he needs to at night.

What will I do at work?

If you can, you should pump your breasts at work on breaks and during your lunch hour. Save your milk to give the babysitter the next day. Carry a small cooler or keep it in a refrigerator at work.

If you can't or do not want to pump at work, you still might have to take the pump with you for a week or so, to use when your breasts start to get too full. Just pump enough to relieve the fullness. After you do this for a week or so, your breasts will adjust and won't become engorged at work. You may leak some during the adjustment period (page 31).

On weekends and days off you can go back to nursing on demand. Your breasts should adjust to the change, and you will probably have enough milk for your baby without having to use supplements. If you do not leave your own milk for the baby, your doctor or WIC counselor can tell you which formula to use. It is helpful to have extra breastmilk (or formula) for the babysitter in case of an emergency.

How do I pump and store milk?

There may be times when you have to be away from your baby. You can still leave breastmilk for him.

Most mothers don't need a breast pump. You can successfully nurse your baby without ever using one. If you are going back to work or school, then you may want to use an electric pump. These are available to buy or rent. For occasional use, a hand pump may be all you need.

Another option is to learn to hand express your milk. Once you learn how, it is easy and free. Just place your thumb on top of your breast, just above the areola, with your fingers below and gently squeeze toward the nipple. At first, you may only see a few drops, but as your milk lets down, it will begin to spray. When the milk stops flowing, move your hand to another part of the areola and continue hand expressing.

To collect milk, pump between feedings, or in the morning when you have an abundant supply. Always collect milk in a clean container. You don't have to collect it all at once. Keep a bottle of expressed milk in the refrigerator, and add to it throughout the day. When you have 2-4 ounces, put it in a bottle or breastmilk storage bag and freeze it. Be sure to write the date on it. Use the oldest first.

Fresh breastmilk can be kept 8 hours at room temperature, for 5 days in the refrigerator and up to 2 weeks in the freezer section of a one-door refrigerator. It will keep 3 months in the freezer section of a two-door refrigerator and up to 12 months in a deep freezer.

Frozen breastmilk should be thawed out under warm running water. Never thaw it out in a microwave because it will destroy some of the important nutrients and it could burn your baby's mouth.

What if I have to leave formula?

Some mothers find that they are just too tired or stressed out to completely breastfeed while they are working. Pumping is a big commitment, and worth the effort, but don't feel guilty if you find you can't do it. It doesn't have to be an "all or nothing" thing. Even nursing part time will help you give the best to your baby.

If you do plan to leave formula instead of breastmilk, make sure the baby can take it long before you return to work. Some babies are allergic to cow milk formula and have to be given soy formula. Your baby's doctor or WIC breastfeeding counselor can tell you which formula to give.

What are my choices?

Most mothers don't have a choice, but if you *do* have a choice about going back to work, think long and hard before you decide. Your baby will miss you, and you will miss your baby. No one can really take your place.

Consider all the extra expenses you will have when you work. Babysitters, new clothes, eating out, convenience foods, and car expenses can really add up. Subtract all of these expenses from your salary and see if it is really worth it. You might be surprised just how little you have left.

If staying home with your baby is important to you, look at your expenses and decide what you can live without. Can you keep your old car a while longer, eat less convenience foods, or find a cheaper place to live? Can your family help out for awhile?

There are also many jobs that can be done from home. Babysitting other children can be a good way to earn money, and your child will always have a playmate.

Your baby will not be a baby very long, and the first few years are so important to his well-being. You will not regret staying at home with your child.

What type of breast pump should I use?

There are many breasts pumps to choose from. Choosing a pump to suit your needs is not easy. Ask a lactation consultant or your WIC counselor to help you decide. Some WIC offices have electric pumps that you can borrow. Breast pumps vary by size and how they are powered.

• With a manual pump, *you* supply the power, either by squeezing handles or by pushing and pulling a cylinder.

• Pumps that have a rubber bulb that you squeeze are hard to control the suction and may damage your nipples.

• One type of manual pump can be converted to a pedal pump. Your foot works a pedal like an old fashioned sewing machine.

• Small battery/electric pumps can either be automatic or require you to control the suction rhythm with your finger. The biggest complaint with battery operated pumps is the short life span of the batteries. The suction gets less and less as the batteries get weaker. Check the warranty before you buy a battery pump. You can buy a small pump to use once in a while, but they won't hold up if you work full time and plan to use it every day. Most of the battery-operated pumps can be converted to electric with the use of an adapter.

• The larger electric pumps are expensive, so mothers usually rent these instead of buying. Some have battery packs, which makes them more portable. Many WIC clinics have electric pumps to loan if you and your baby must be separated due to illness or if you are working.

Pumping both breasts at the same time is handy for mothers who need to pump in a hurry. This also stimulates your milk supply better. You can do this by using two one-handed manual pumps, a pedal pump, or a large electric pump.

A good pump is comfortable to use and does not hurt. When you first use a pump, you may not get much milk. You might only cover the bottom of the bottle. But pumping gets better with practice! Ten to fifteen minutes is long enough to pump. If you are trying to build up your milk supply, pump more often, not longer. Massaging your breasts and hand expressing milk are both good ways to help your milk letdown while pumping.

Massaging your breasts is easy. Gently stroke your breasts with your fingertips, as if you are doing a breast self-exam. Keep moving to a new place until you have massaged the whole breast. Compressing your breast gently with your fingers or shaking your breast will also help your milk let down.

When you pump or express one breast at a time, change from one breast to the other as the flow of milk slows down. Switch back and forth several times in a pumping session. Stress can make it harder for you to letdown your milk. If you can, find some peace and quiet for yourself when you pump or express.

How do I hand express my milk?

The very best way to collect breastmilk for your baby is to *hand express* it. No pump is needed at all. Hand expression empties the breast better than a pump, so it helps maintain your milk supply better. Some women even learn to hand express faster than an electric pump. Here's how:

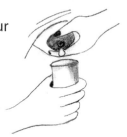

• First, massage the breast.

• Put your thumb above the nipple and the fingers below at the edge of the areola, the dark area around the nipple, about 1 1/2 inches from the base of the nipple.

• Press your finger and thumb into the breast toward your ribs. Then press them toward each other and roll toward the nipple, without sliding your fingers over the skin. Then release the pressure and repeat several times.

You may just see a drop at first. Keep doing it, and soon milk will start to drip. Finally, it will begin to spray out in several streams. When the flow of milk slows, turn your hand so that your fingers and thumb can reach all the way around the areola. Then switch to the other breast. You can use both hands on both breasts or even express both at once by leaning over two containers.

WHEN TO ASK FOR HELP
You may need help if:

- you have flat or inverted nipples.
- you are heavily engorged.
- your baby doesn't latch on.
- your baby has colic.
- your baby has thrush.
- your nipples get sore or cracked.
- your breasts hurt.
- you have a plugged duct.
- you have a breast infection.
- you don't seem to be making enough milk.
- your baby is not having enough wet diapers.
- your baby is not having enough bowel movements.
- your baby is not gaining weight.

12
Where to Turn for Help

Don't give up, ask for help if you are having problems with breastfeeding.

What is WIC?

The Special Supplemental Nutrition Program for Women, Infants, and Children (WIC) provides nutrition education, breastfeeding promotion and support, referrals to health care, and supplemental foods to pregnant and postpartum women, and to infants and children up to age 5.

Since the goal of WIC is to have healthy mothers and children, they provide some of the foods needed for good health. WIC checks, good for certain healthy foods only, are given to pregnant and postpartum mothers and used in grocery stores. Formula is given to those who choose to bottle feed.

To be eligible, you and your baby must need extra food to be healthy, and you must meet certain income standards. You also have to live in an area that has a WIC clinic, and you have to go there for regular appointments.

WIC employees know how important breastfeeding is to growing babies and they will do all they can to help you succeed. Some WIC offices have special Breastfeeding Peer Counselors. They are mothers who have breastfed and are trained to help you. Some WIC offices also have lactation consultants to help you.

Don't be afraid to ask WIC for help if you have problems breastfeeding. They want you to enjoy your baby and keep him healthy by breastfeeding a long time.

If you are not already on WIC, call your local Health Department for more details. They can tell you where and how to apply.

What is the WIC Peer Counseling Program?

Peer Counselors are women who have breastfed their babies. They have been trained to help other women learn to breastfeed. Peer Counselors have 20 hours of training to learn more about breastfeeding and how to help others. After the training, they are certified to counsel breastfeeding mothers.

Peer Counselors help mothers in lots of ways. They promote breastfeeding at pregnancy and WIC clinics and work with Health Departments. Some start breastfeeding support groups or even work with mothers on a one-to-one basis by making phone calls, and home or hospital visits.

Breastfeeding Peer Counseling Programs are started by WIC Breastfeeding Coordinators who have completed special training for this work.

What is La Leche League?

La Leche League International is the world's authority on breastfeeding. It was started in 1956 by a group of nursing mothers and now has groups all over the world.

Mothers and their nursing babies meet once a month to talk about the benefits of breastfeeding, the baby's first few days, overcoming problems and starting solids and weaning. These meetings give mothers a chance to talk about their feelings and problems they are having. They leave the meetings grateful for finding other mothers much like them. Many lasting friendships begin at La Leche League meetings.

A qualified Leader conducts the meeting and helps answer questions. Groups have large lending libraries with parenting books and videos. La Leche League Leaders give free phone help and are happy to share their breastfeeding knowledge. They don't give medical advice. If they can't help you, they will refer you to someone who can.

For more information or to find a local meeting, contact:

La Leche League International
P. O. Box 4079, Schaumburg, IL 60168
1-800-LA-LECHE | www.lalecheleague.org

What is an International Board Certified Lactation Consultant (IBCLC)?

An IBCLC is a paid, professional health worker who helps mothers learn to breastfeed and overcome problems. They work in hospitals, public health clinics, doctors' offices and private practices. Some teach breastfeeding classes and offer telephone support.

IBCLCs have been trained in lactation and have taken an exam to become certified. All are professionals who have a great deal of hands-on experience helping mothers.

IBCLCs are the newest members of the healthcare team. They work as a team with other healthcare workers who help breastfeeding mothers.

For more information or to find an IBCLC in your area, contact:

International Lactation Consultant Association
500 Sunday Drive, Suite 102, Raleigh, NC 27607
919-861-5577 | www.ilca.org

INDEX

AIDS 36
After pains 15
Alcohol 46
Alertness 11
Allergies 4, 41, 52
Antibiotics 36, 43
Antibodies 4, 20, 36, 51
Areola 7

Bilirubin 39
Birth control 37
Biting 25
Bonding 1
Bowel movements 19, 23, 39, 42
Bras 31
Breast(s)
     cancer 3
     infection 33
     massage 34, 59, 60
     milk production 7, 11
     pads 31
     prenatal care 5
     structure 7
Breastfeeding
     advantages 1-3
     aids 29
     discreetly 26
     during night 21
     first time 11
     for comfort 1, 42
     frequency 17
     how long 18
     positions 12-13
     preparation for 5
Breastmilk jaundice 39
Breast pumps 29, 56, 58
Breast shells 6, 30
Burping 20

Caffeine 41, 46
Cereal 21, 50

Cesarean section 12, 13, 34
Cluster Feed 18
Colic 41
Colostrum 5, 11
Constipation 24, 42
Crib death 4
Crying 17, 21

Dental problems 1
Diarrhea 1, 23
Diet
     Mother's 45-46
     Baby's 49
Discreet nursing 26
Drugs 36, 47

Emotional needs 2, 21
Engorgement 33
Eyes 1
Expressing milk
     at work 56
     breast pumps 56
     by hand 60

Fathers 25
Flat nipples 6
Foremilk 8-9
Formula 4, 20, 57

Growth spurt 23

Hand expression 60
Hindmilk 8-9
HIV+ 36
Hormones 2, 7-8

Illness
     of baby 42
     of mother 36
Inverted nipples 6
IQ 1

Jaundice 11, 39-40

Lactation Consultant 65
Latch-on 14-15
La Leche League 64
Length of feeds 18
Leaking 31
"Letdown" 8, 31

Marijuana 47
Medication 36
Menstrual periods 3, 36
Milk
    cow 20, 50
    ducts 7
    glands 7
    ejection reflex 8

Nighttime feedings 21
Nipples
    breaking suction 15
    confusion 43
    flat or inverted 6
    shields 30
    sore 35
Nursing (see breastfeeding)
Nursing strike 24
Nursing supplementer 32
Nutrition 45-46

Ovulation 3, 37
Oxytocin 7-8

Pacifier 22
Peer Counselor 64
Pillows 12-13
Plugged duct 33
Portability of babies 2
Positioning
    cradle hold 12
    cross- crade hold 12
    football hold 13
    lying down 13
    twins 16

Pregnancy 5, 37
Premature babies 42
Prolactin 2, 7

Recreational drugs 47
Rooming-in 12

Sleeping 21
Smoking 46
Solid foods 49-51
Sore nipples
    breast shells 6, 30
    preventing 5
    treatment 35
Soybean formula 20
Speech 1
"Spoiling" baby 21
Sucking correctly 7
Supply and demand 7, 16

Teeth 1
Teething 21, 24
Thrush 43
Toddlers 52
Twins 16

Uterus 3, 15

Water 20
Weaning 24, 51-53
Weight gain of baby 4, 8, 18, 27
Weight loss of mother 3, 45
Wet diapers 19
WIC 63-64
Working & Breastfeeding 55-60

About the Author
PAMELA K. WIGGINS, IBCLC

Pam has been helping breastfeeding moms for almost thirty years.

Pamela King Wiggins is an International Board Certified Lactation Consultant. Considered one of the pioneers, she made the trek to Washington, D.C. to take the very first IBCLC examination in 1985. She served as a La Leche League leader for many years.

She teaches breastfeeding classes to expectant parents and presents in-services for nurses. She has previously worked for WIC, where she designed and initiated a lactation program in a Florida hospital. She has been counseling breastfeeding mothers for almost three decades.

Pamela is a member of the International Lactation Consultant Association, the Tidewater Area Lactation Consultant Association and La Leche League International and various other breastfeeding advocacy groups.

She is also the author of *Breastfeeding: A Mother's Gift*, another popular breastfeeding guide, *Dad's 10 Minute Breastfeeding Guide*, *Breastfeeding During Emergencies*, and *Life in the Family Lane*, a collection of humorous and heart-warming essays taken from her popular magazine column of the same name. She has recently produced a DVD, *Breastfeeding: You Can Do It!*

The author and her husband have three children and six grandchildren (all nursed.) They live on a farm where they grow peanuts & pine trees.

Other Products by Pamela K. Wiggins, IBCLC:

Breastfeeding: You Can Do It! (DVD)

A DVD designed & priced to be given to parents. The quality is outstanding. It is thorough, up-to-date, evidence based & features 30 different families of various ethnicities. It teaches why it is important to breastfeed & how to do it.

All DVDs have 4 videos in English & Spanish: Breastfeeding: You Can Do It!; Breastfeeding: Getting Started; Self Attachment; and Frequently Asked Questions. Available in a Bulk, Classroom/Retail or a Looped Institutional Version.

(39 min total time, All Grade Levels, 2007, English & Spanish)

Easy to read and mother friendly. Includes asymmetrical latch-on, reverse pressure softening, newborn stomach sizes, attachment parenting, co-sleeping guidelines & the most extensive list of referenced advantages of any book.

Foreword by Katherine Dettwyler, PhD. Medications section by Dr. Tom Hale. Appendix includes Breastfeeding During Emergencies & A Note to Expectant Dads. Photographs & illustrations of mothers and babies of several ethnic groups.

(160 pages, 7th Grade Level, Revised 2006, English & Spanish)

Breastfeeding: A Mother's Gift

Dad's 10 Minute Breastfeeding Guide

There are many choices when baby is on the way, but the amount of information can be overwhelming. An informed & supportive father can make a great impact on a mother's breastfeeding success.

This basic guide can be read in a few minutes. It teaches the advantages of breastfeeding, the risks of formula, what to expect the first few weeks & how to help. This resolves concerns dads may have about breastfeeding.

(8 Color Pages, 6th Grade Level, Revised 2007, English & Spanish)

All moms should be encouraged to breastfeed, it is best for the baby and mom. But what does a mom do during a disaster? Formula or fresh water may not be available.

Designed for moms, this explains why breastfeeding is crucial during emergencies, how to continue breastfeeding during a disaster & how to relactate if necessary. Emphasizes that babies can be completely sustained on breastmilk for the first 6 months.

(8 Color Pages, 6th Grade Level, Revised 2007, English & Spanish)

Breastfeeding During Emergencies

For more information or to order any of these products contact:
LA PUBLISHING, LLC
P.O. Box 773 Franklin, VA 23851
800-397-5833 804-744-6022 (Fax)
www.breastfeedingbooks.com
Providing Quality Products to Educate Parents about Breastfeeding